ALL SAINTS

Icons of the Twelve Parish Saints of Jersey

"All my delight is in your Saints.

The faithful who dwell in your land.

The lines have fallen for me in pleasant places.

I have been given a welcome heritage."

Psalm 16

Karen Blampied

First published Jersey 2011 by The Heritage Trust

Design by The Idea Works, Jersey

Text © Karen Blampied

Photographs © Mehdi Padidar, Steven Achler & Roger Sebire

Illustrations © Karen Blampied

ISBN 978-0-9562079-4-4

Contents

Acknowledgements

The author thanks and acknowledges the contributions made by;

Mehdi Padidar for icon photographs.

Steven Achler for Parish Church photographs.

Roger Sebire for the photograph of the statue of Saint Helier.

Angela Le Sueur & Gio Pollano for proof reading the text.

'The Idea Works' for the attention to detail in the design.

Doug Ford of Jersey Heritage for his historical knowledge.

Lord Coutanche Library Staff for their help with research.

Sr Petra Clare of Sancti Angeli Skete for giving me the idea.

Yvonne Callec for focusing my ideas and translating the French texts.

Enid and Jeff Blampied my parents for their enthusiastic support.

The Very Reverend Robert Key, all the Parish Church Rectors and the Anglican Church
community for welcoming me into their churches as artist-in-residence.

*All Saints - Icons of the Twelve Parish Saints of Jersey, has been most generously
sponsored by Veronica Langlois in memory of her parents A.G. (Fred) and Mary Langlois.*

Foreword

By The Very Reverend R.F. Key B.A, Dean of Jersey

During 2010 Karen Blampied set out on a pilgrimage around the twelve ancient Parish Churches of Jersey and like all pilgrimages she had a religious purpose to her journey. Karen chose to 'make visible' through the writing of icons the Twelve Parish Saints whose names define the map of Jersey, thereby encountering these 'Saints' as sacred people of purpose, not just as place names. As Rowan Williams, Archbishop of Canterbury points out in his book 'The Dwelling of the Light: Praying with Icons of Christ': 'In the icon, what you see is human beings and situations as they are in the light of God's action.'

There has been a tremendous increase in the appreciation of sacred icons in the West during the last 20 years. The Orthodox Church teaches that the 'sacred image' has existed from the beginning of Christianity. Therefore, any contemporary iconographer must rediscover the true essential tradition of the iconographers of old, be faithful to this tradition yet speak the language of today. Through the icons and annotated sketches found in this book, the language of the icon enables a dynamic encounter with the Parish Saints of Jersey through their personal stories, and through the statements of faith their lives personify.

God speaks to us through the wonder of creation, His infallible word in the Holy Scriptures and, supremely, in His Son the Lord Jesus Christ. I pray that these icons may be vehicles of God's loving call to us to follow, as the hymn puts it, "Where the saints have trod."

Robert Key
Dean of Jersey

Islands at a Crossroads of Belief

Doug Ford of Jersey Heritage

Tradition has it that most of the Parish Churches in the Island have their foundation in the eleventh century, however, this may simply be because the parochial structure was reorganised at this time. Some of the church sites are most certainly older.

Established during the late Roman period the Christian Church came under extreme pressure during the last days of the Empire from the violent incursions of the Germanic tribes. At this time the organisation of the Church was still being formulated and there were a number of competing interpretations or choices to be made – this is the original meaning of the term heresy before it came to mean someone whose beliefs were different from the accepted doctrines.

As the Empire collapsed the Church on the mainland took over the imperial bureaucracy and became centred around bishops and dioceses owing allegiance to the central authority of the Pope in Rome. The links between Christian Britain and the Continent became very tenuous and tended to be with missionaries from Western Gaul who were heavily influenced by the eremitical monastic movement. The result of this was that a native British Church evolved during the 5th and 6th centuries and became increasingly insular in form, being largely clan or tribal dominated, and loosely based around monasteries ruled by hereditary abbots.

This insular form of Christianity was in reality a loose confederation of semi-autonomous churches for unlike the Roman tradition of Christianity there was no central authority such as the Pope nor was there a rigid doctrine, therefore, the Celtic Church was open to all forms of influences or heresies - Arian, Athanasian, Pelagian. Personal interpretation of the Bible provided the doctrine. This uniquely British Celtic form of Christianity led to the flowering and spread, by wandering holy men or "saints" as they were known, of Celtic monasticism and learning so important in the 6th, 7th and 8th centuries. Travelling extensively between Ireland, South Wales, Cornwall, the Channel Islands and Brittany, obviously these missionary ways can be plotted by using place name evidence and church dedications.

The successes of the Germanic tribes in Northern and Eastern Britain led to many Britons forsaking their homeland and seeking refuge amongst their Celtic kinsfolk in Armorica.

This migration was on such a scale that the region became known as Little Britain or Brittany because its character was so drastically altered.

The Channel Islands were very much a crossroads of these two Christian traditions – the insular British and the mainland Roman and this is reflected in the insular dedications.

The evidence on the ground is rather thin but, what there is, is important: the 7th and 8th century eremitic monastic site at the Ile Agois in St Mary, the monastic community set up following the death of St Helier in AD 555 on the Islet in St Aubin's Bay, the circular enclosure of St Brelade's Church, an early carved fish emblem reused in the walls of St Mary's Church and perhaps the greatest enigma of this Dark Age the 6th century dedication to a British priest on the St Lawrence Stone found beneath the nave of the Parish Church during restoration work in the 1890s.

With the growth of centralised authority in the person of the king in the developing kingdoms of the Franks and the English during the Dark Ages, this idea of an individualistic, semi-autonomous Church posed problems. The Roman tradition of dioceses, bishops and archbishops appeared to be easier to influence, therefore, in the first decade of the 9th century the Emperor Charlemagne who laid claim to the Channel Islands dispatched St Gervold, Abbot of Fontenelle, to Jersey on "Imperial business". This would appear to have been a mission to bring the Church on the Island into the mainstream Roman tradition and to break away from the Breton Church. In this he would appear to have been successful, however, this was probably short lived as the 9th and 10th centuries saw the political cohesion of the North-West of France smashed by pagan Norse raiders and settlers.

By the time the newly settled Norse adventurers annexed the Cotentin and the Islands in AD 933 they had nominally been converted to the mainstream Roman tradition. When their 11th century Norman descendants reorganised the parochial structure of the Islands they tied the churches in with mainland Norman religious foundations but their dedications reflect an earlier devotion to the Channel Islands' earlier Christian traditions.

Saint Mary of the Burnt Monastery

Mary is an icon of motherhood within the Christian faith. Her story is that of a young woman chosen by God to be the Mother of Jesus. Visited by the angel Gabriel she says 'Yes' to this request, humbly securing for herself a major role in the Christian history of human salvation. Throughout the Bible we find her at all the key moments in her Son's life, death and resurrection. She is portrayed as a tender loving mother encouraging her Son to live out His purpose to build the Kingdom of God.

Mary the Mother of Jesus is therefore seen by Christians as a saint for her part in the Christian story. The church that is dedicated to her name, Saint Mary of the Burnt Monastery, tells its own story of Christian witness. As the name suggests there was a link to a monastery in that area of the Parish of St Mary or perhaps the then neighbouring monastic centre in Sark.

The Parish Church of Saint Mary of the Burnt Monastery.

Writing an icon of St Mary of the Burnt Monastery

Despite the complexity of the subject I needed to keep the icon simple and yet show Mary's role in the Christian plan of salvation.

Iconography has a wealth of images in relation to Mary. For this reason I chose those that would begin to interpret visually 'Saint Mary of the Burnt Monastery'.

I depict Mary enthroned with the monastery on her lap engulfed by flames. In the middle of the burning monastery, is Christ as Emmanuel (God-with-us); the Christ Child of Christmas, Incarnate, the Word that was made flesh and dwelt among us. Mary's right hand points to Christ, reminding the onlooker that it is Christ who is at the centre of this icon. The colours within the icon are symbolic: her blue robe symbolises her part in the divine plan of salvation and the red outer garment (maphorian) is a symbol of her humanity. Christ wears the colours of 'Emmanuel' - orange and white whose golden glow symbolises His powerful, divine energy.

SAINT MARY OF

THE BURNT MONASTERY

Icons of Mary

Within the canon of iconography, Mary is represented through several prototypes.

Our Lady of the Sign
This prototype finds its inspiration from Scripture. (Isaiah 7:4): "The Lord himself will give you a sign: the virgin will be with child and she will give birth to a son who will be called God-with-us, Emmanuel."

Our Lady who Shows the Way
This is a classic Byzantine prototype – Hodegetria – meaning 'She who Shows the Way' which is referred to by the Akathistos hymn "Greetings, thou who showeth the way to those who walk in darkness." In this icon the right hand of Mary is positioned so that it points towards her Son, indicating the New Testament verse in John 14:6: "I am the way the truth and the life."

Our Lady of the Burning Bush
This prototype is inspired by the Old Testament story of Moses at the Burning Bush, a bush that was not consumed by its own flames. This was interpreted by the Fathers of the Church as an image of Mary, who bore Christ, the Divine Fire.

Our Lady Enthroned
This prototype emphasis the royalty of the Mother of God. The throne thus becomes a metaphor of the Virgin Mother of God who is the true temple of the Holy Spirit, the dwelling place of God.

Each of these offers an aspect relevant to an icon that depicts the church's name, Saint Mary of the Burnt Monastery. The emphasis in this icon is on the role Mary played in the plan of salvation.

An annotated sketch of the icon of Saint Mary of the Burnt Monastery

In the halo of the Christ Child are the letters WON - meaning: 'I am who I am'. (Exodus 3:14) The response which Moses receives at the Burning Bush.

The three stars which appear on Mary's head and shoulders symbolise her virginity before, during and after giving birth to Jesus. 'Hail Mary full of Grace.' These symbolise the grace-filled moments in Mary's life.

The Christ Child within the medallion of the burning monastery expresses the belief that: 'The God in heaven will set up a Kingdom which shall never be destroyed.' (Dn 2:44)

In the iconographic prototype, Our Lady of the Sign, the monastery forms the medallion. Mary is the one who encloses the Divine and becomes its transparence. A Byzantine hymn says: 'Your womb is more vast than the heavens for it encompasses the One the heavens could not.'

The right hand of the Christ Child is raised in a blessing showing His humanity and divinity. His left hand holds a scroll: the Word of God.

In the iconographic prototype, Mother of God Enthroned, the red cushioned ornate throne is a symbol of Mary's royalty.

The iconographic prototype, Virgin of the Burning Bush, links the New Testament with Old Testament prophecies of the coming of salvation in which Mary would have a key role.

The flames engulf the burning monastery as the name of the Parish Church expresses.

The lily of the Annunciation, the 'Fleur de Lys,' a flower associated with Mary and used as the Parish Crest.

The Christ Child is robed as the Emmanuel, referring to the Church as a historical reality and yet transcending history. 'For to us a child is born, to us a son is given. The Lord himself will give you a sign. Behold a young woman shall conceive and bear a son, and shall call his name Emmanuel.' (Isaiah 9:6; 7:14)

The ladder placed like this in an icon of Mary is a sign of the unity between heaven and earth brought to fruition by the Incarnation. It leads redeemed humanity heavenwards.

The ladder is also a symbol which goes back to Jacob's vision in the Old Testament. 'Hail heavenly ladder down which came God; Hail transfer bridge for earthlings to heaven.' (Akathistos hymn.)

In the iconographic prototype, Our Lady who Shows the Way, the hand of Mary points to Christ her Son, indicating: 'He is the Way the Truth and the Light.' (John 14:6) This is the crux of Christian iconography.

Traditionally in iconography Mary wears a red maphorion expressing her humanity. She is a human creature who bore in her womb the Son of God. Mary's blue robe is a symbol of her part in the divine plan.

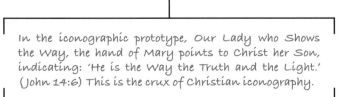

Saint John of the Oaks

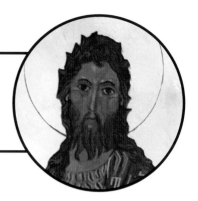

The church of Saint John of the Oaks is named after Saint John the Baptist, Jesus' cousin. It is situated in the middle of St John's Village surrounded by trees, possibly the reason why the church was given the name 'of the Oaks'. Whatever the reason, the image gives great scope for interpretation.

In terms of the biblical story, John is the son of Zechariah and Elizabeth a cousin of Mary. We first encounter John as a baby in the womb of his mother, and we are told by Luke that he leaps for joy at the meeting between Elizabeth and Mary who is carrying Jesus in her womb.

Probably having known each other since childhood, there seems to be a gentle yet profound understanding between John and Jesus when they encounter each other again on the banks of the River Jordan.

"Jesus came from Galilee to John at the Jordan, to be baptised by him. John would have prevented him saying, 'I need to be baptised by you.' But Jesus answered him; 'Let it be so now; for it is proper for us in this way to fulfil all righteousness.'" (Matt 3:13-15)

This baptism gives John a key role in Jesus' life and marks the historical beginning of Jesus' ministry.

John's incredible story of martyrdom can be found in Scripture. His life ended around AD27 with his head being presented to King Herod on a plate at the request of Salome, Herod's daughter. (Mark 6:28)

Within the Eastern Orthodox Church, John is known as John the Forerunner. As one of the central figures in Christian history his mission was one of forerunner and herald to Jesus Christ. There are several icon prototypes of John the Baptist: Angel of the Desert, Precursor of Christ, Prophet and Saint. The icon of Saint John of the Oaks uses aspects from all of these icons.

The Parish Church of Saint John of the Oaks.

Writing an icon of St John

My challenge was to interpret all the information about John into an icon. I wanted to include the idea 'of the Oaks' so I included the stylized tree image as found in Orthodox icons and also the axe lodged in one of the trees. This emphasises John's words as found in the New Testament: 'Even now the axe is lying at the root of the trees; every tree therefore that does not bear good fruit is cut down and thrown into the fire'. (Matt 3:10)

I chose to emphasise John's teaching and preaching through his hands. His right hand is raised in the gesture of an orator while in the other he holds a scroll. This symbolises the Word of God that he preached. It is placed at the centre of the icon because it was at the centre of his mission.

John's clothing is clearly described in Scripture, and so he wears the ascetic hides of an animal. But he also wears a Jewish prayer shawl, the tallit, around his waist to show the Jewish nature of his message as written by the prophet Isaiah: "A voice cries out in the wilderness, 'Prepare the way of the Lord, make straight in the desert a highway for our God.'" (Isaiah 40:3)

John stands next to the River Jordan reminiscent of the baptism of repentance that he offered the people of Judea. 'They were baptised by him in the River Jordan, confessing their sins. "I baptise you with water, but one more powerful than I is coming after me. I am not worthy to undo his sandals. He will baptise you with the Holy Spirit and fire." (Matt 3:6&11) It was here that John baptised Jesus.

John's feet are indicative of his purpose and mission to 'Make straight the path of the Lord'. In iconography John prepares the way for Christ. He is the last of the old-style prophets of the Old Testament; his stark message is one of repentance. John's life marks the end of the old promise and the beginning of the new promise. He is a bridge between the God of the Old Testament and New Testament. He was the last prophet and first saint.

The main emphasis of this icon is to show that John was 'A voice crying in the wilderness'. So the setting of this icon is a deserted hilltop, symbolising the 'wilderness' of the soul that has forgotten the language of repentance.

An annotated sketch of Saint John of the Oaks

Saint John of the Oaks. The stylized trees echo the nature of this Parish Saint. He was a man of nature feeding on locusts and wild honey.

The stylized trees and the axe that will cut down the trees that do not produce good fruit. John preached repentance to sinners and encouraged them to bear good fruit by the things they do in life. The tree that bears good fruit will prosper.

John's right hand spells the name of Christ ICXC. It is held in this position to show that he is an orator and his purpose is to preach the way of the Lord. An Eastern Orthodox prayer states: 'May your hand, O Baptist which touched the head of the Lord, and which pointed out to us that he was the Saviour, be extended towards him in our favour.'

The garment John wears shows his austere lifestyle, a camel hair fleece in the desert. His belt, a tallit, shows his Jewish upbringing.

'Even now the axe is laid to the roots of the trees so that any tree which fails to produce good fruit will be cut down and thrown into the fire.' (Matt 3) The axe that slew the Baptist because his message called into question the moral life of those who said they believed.

'Prepare a way for the Lord, make straight his path.' (Matt 3:3) The left foot slopes down on uneven rock whereas his right foot makes straight the way.

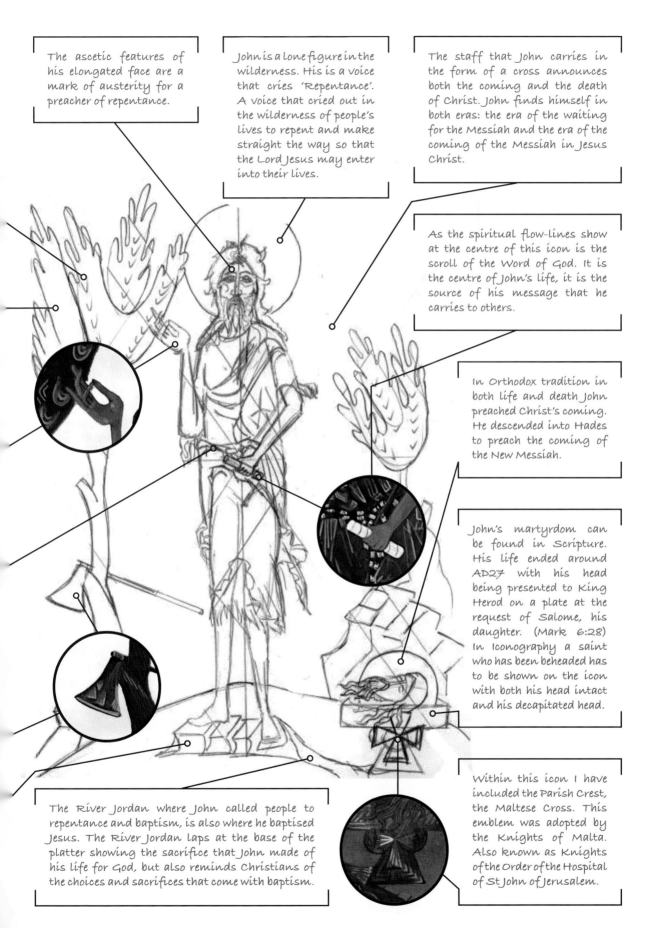

The ascetic features of his elongated face are a mark of austerity for a preacher of repentance.

John is a lone figure in the wilderness. His is a voice that cries 'Repentance'. A voice that cried out in the wilderness of people's lives to repent and make straight the way so that the Lord Jesus may enter into their lives.

The staff that John carries in the form of a cross announces both the coming and the death of Christ. John finds himself in both eras: the era of the waiting for the Messiah and the era of the coming of the Messiah in Jesus Christ.

As the spiritual flow-lines show at the centre of this icon is the scroll of the Word of God. It is the centre of John's life, it is the source of his message that he carries to others.

In Orthodox tradition in both life and death John preached Christ's coming. He descended into Hades to preach the coming of the New Messiah.

John's martyrdom can be found in Scripture. His life ended around AD27 with his head being presented to King Herod on a plate at the request of Salome, his daughter. (Mark 6:28) In Iconography a saint who has been beheaded has to be shown on the icon with both his head intact and his decapitated head.

The River Jordan where John called people to repentance and baptism, is also where he baptised Jesus. The River Jordan laps at the base of the platter showing the sacrifice that John made of his life for God, but also reminds Christians of the choices and sacrifices that come with baptism.

Within this icon I have included the Parish Crest, the Maltese Cross. This emblem was adopted by the Knights of Malta. Also known as Knights of the Order of the Hospital of St John of Jerusalem.

Saint Saviour of Jersey

In Christian belief Jesus Christ was the 'Anointed One' of God whose mission was to establish the Kingdom of God on earth. Christ Jesus, Son of God, born of the Virgin Mary became incarnate. He was the human and divine key to God's plan of salvation for all people.

His human existence in history was recorded by writers of the Roman ruling power at the time. He was born just before the death of Herod the Great in 4BC and was executed by crucifixion around 30AD after being condemned to death by Pontius Pilate, Governor of Judea 26AD-36AD. Christians believe that through His life, death and resurrection He saved humankind from the power of evil. That is why He is often referred to as the 'Saviour of the World'.

The church and Parish of Saint Saviour celebrate the Patronal Feast Day of Christ the King. This is a celebration of the all-embracing authority of Christ within the Church to lead people to the Kingdom of God, through the 'peace of Christ.' The Parish Crest is the Crown of Thorns and nails; this has resulted from the name of Saint Sauveur de l'Epine being used at some time in its history.

The Orthodox tradition believes that because Christ Jesus became incarnate His image can now be made for all to see through the icon. According to Leonid Ouspensky: 'The (Orthodox) Church declares that the icon is an outcome of the Incarnation.' The icon is faith made visible. This is why within the icon tradition there are many prototypes of the Saviour. He can be represented as: 'Emmanuel'; the Christ Child of the Nativity; as 'Not made by human hands,' from the famous Edessa cloth on which the face of Christ was said to have been imprinted; as the 'Saviour of the Universe'; as 'King of Kings'; as the 'True Vine' and many more. All of these give us an insight into Christian belief about Christ Jesus, The Saviour.

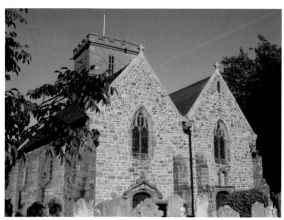

The Parish Church of Saint Saviour of Jersey.

Writing an icon of St Saviour of Jersey

To interpret all these statements of faith about Christ Jesus into a single icon was a challenge. I wanted to express 'The Saviour's' eternal presence, as well as His historical purpose and theological impact.

The angels link the Old Testament Book of Genesis with the New Testament Gospel of Mark. It was the angels who banished Adam from Paradise and the angels who protected Christ in the wilderness. Here, the angels show Christ Jesus as the New Adam, not giving into temptation and so establishing the New Covenant for humankind.

In keeping with the Feast of Christ the King I chose to represent The Saviour as Pantocrator, Seat of Wisdom. Here the Saviour is seated on a throne, holding in his left hand the Scriptures, the cover of which shows the Parish Crest of the Crown of Thorns and nails reminding us of Christ's Passion. The throne is also to be interpreted as 'the seat of judgement,' echoing the belief in the Second Coming: 'He will come again to judge the living and the dead and His kingdom will have no end.'

I wanted to interpret visually Christ's divine transcendence through His garments. The dark blue tunic is highlighted with rays of light, to show how Christ's divine strength sheds light on human reality. As Saint Athanasius wrote; 'The omnipotent and most holy WORD of the Father, penetrating all things and reaching everywhere with His strength, gives light to all reality.'

The Lamb, a symbol used by the church community of Saint Saviour, is Christ's footstool in the icon, reminding us that He was the Paschal Lamb slain for all offences. The Divine Office Hymn for Christ the King proclaims: 'Hail Redeemer, King divine, Priest and Lamb the throne is thine. King whose reign shall never cease, Prince of everlasting peace.'

An annotated sketch of Saint Saviour of Jersey

The head of Christ is surrounded by a crossed halo, in which is inscribed the Greek letters OWN – an abbreviation for the present participle of the Greek verb 'to be' – i.e. 'The one who is being.' 'I am who I am,' (Exodus 3:14) the answer Moses receives at the Burning Bush, link the Old Testament declaration with the person of Christ.

The angels link Genesis with the Gospel of Mark, Old and New Testaments. The angels who banished Adam from Paradise protect Jesus in the wilderness. Jesus is the New Adam, the New Promise. They are in a gesture of protecting Jesus.

His right hand is raised in a gesture of blessing, spelling His name and indicating His human and divine nature. The Trinity, God the Father, Son and Holy Spirit is symbolised through the position of the fingers.

The dark blue tunic is decorated with fine gold ochre strips of paint over a dark red undergarment. Together with the gold background, they are signs of Christ's divinity. They symbolise divine transcendence. The main emphasis of this icon is to show that the reign of God is universal and eternal.

The four feet of the throne symbolise the four corners of the earth.

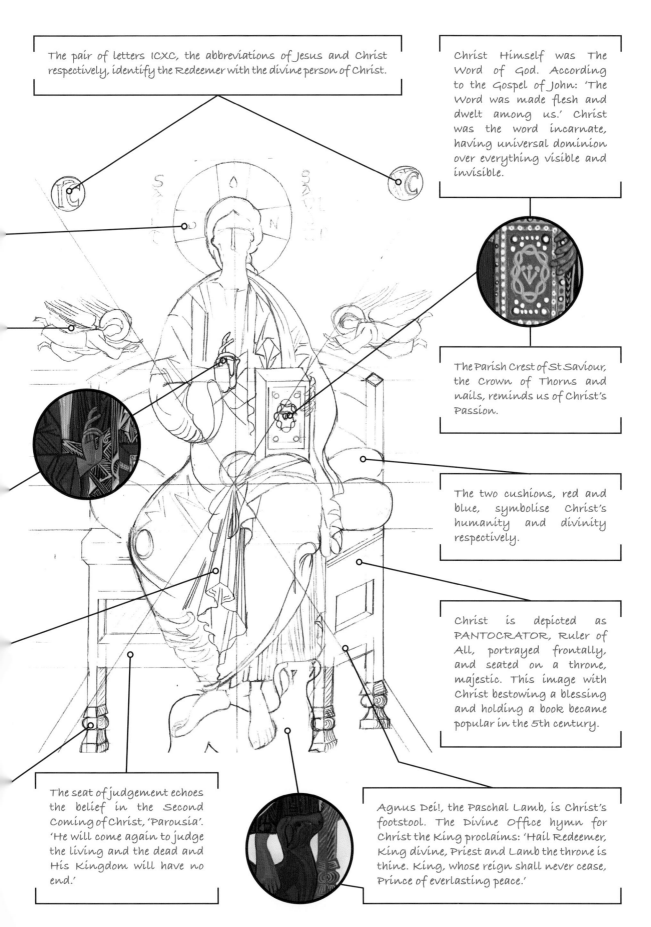

The pair of letters ICXC, the abbreviations of Jesus and Christ respectively, identify the Redeemer with the divine person of Christ.

Christ Himself was The Word of God. According to the Gospel of John: 'The Word was made flesh and dwelt among us.' Christ was the word incarnate, having universal dominion over everything visible and invisible.

The Parish Crest of St Saviour, the Crown of Thorns and nails, reminds us of Christ's Passion.

The two cushions, red and blue, symbolise Christ's humanity and divinity respectively.

Christ is depicted as PANTOCRATOR, Ruler of All, portrayed frontally, and seated on a throne, majestic. This image with Christ bestowing a blessing and holding a book became popular in the 5th century.

The seat of judgement echoes the belief in the Second Coming of Christ, 'Parousia'. 'He will come again to judge the living and the dead and His Kingdom will have no end.'

Agnus Dei!, the Paschal Lamb, is Christ's footstool. The Divine Office hymn for Christ the King proclaims: 'Hail Redeemer, King divine, Priest and Lamb the throne is thine. King, whose reign shall never cease, Prince of everlasting peace.'

Saint Peter in the Desert

The church and Parish of Saint Peter in the Desert are named after the Apostle Peter. As one of the central figures in Christian art and history, his mission was to establish Christ's Church on earth. Peter's story is full of life and meaning and is well documented in Scripture.

Jersey was at the crossroads of Celtic and Roman saints and here in the name 'Saint Peter in the Desert' we have reference to the two differing Christian structures; it is almost as if in this name 'Saint Peter in the Desert' East and West meet.

'Saint Peter' is, within Western Church history, known as the Bishop of Rome, the first Pope. The bureaucratic structure of the Roman Empire was used by the Church in Rome for the hierarchical structure of the Western Church, priests and bishops under the authority of Rome. Saints like Peter spread the popularity of this structure.

'In the Desert,' however, is a reference to the monastic structure which came out of Egypt with Saint Anthony of the Desert (251-356). The term 'desert' came to mean 'monastery' within the Celtic monastic tradition. The monastic structure was monk and abbot who were under a different authority and its popularity spread with Celtic monks like Saint Brelade.

So here we have the Western Roman administrative Church tradition meeting the Eastern monastic tradition: 'Saint Peter in the Desert'. Why this name? It would be interesting to know what was in the mind of the people who named this church community.

Within the writing of the icon, however, I decided to take the name 'Saint Peter in the Desert' in a more literal, biblical sense. Saint Peter was, according to the New Testament, a fisherman, therefore the setting for the icon is a watery desert, and the main focal point is Christ's call to Peter: 'Do not be afraid; from now on it is men you will catch.' (Luke 5:11)

The Parish Church of Saint Peter in the Desert.

SAINT PETER IN THE DESERT

Writing an icon of St Peter in the Desert

My challenge was to interpret all the biblical information about Peter into an icon. I wanted to remain true to the canon of iconography in relation to Peter – his clothes, his stature – but at the same time include the symbolic meaning of his life's work. For this reason I included Peter holding in his right hand the 'Church' which he was invited to build in the name of Jesus Christ. To his left is the symbolic rock, 'pierre,' referring to himself, on which this Church should be built. The desert in reference to the Parish name in this icon is a 'watery' desert. I took my inspiration for this from the 'Five Mile Road' with its dunes and seashore. This led me to include a fishing net draped over Peter's left shoulder, echoing Christ's call to him to be a fisher-of-men.

Also included is a cockerel, a symbol of Peter's struggle to understand his own faith; a faith that overcame all doubt and is an inspiration to us all.

In the top left hand corner we see Christ handing Peter the 'keys'. I therefore was able to include the main aspect of the Parish Crest and draw attention to the fact that Peter was given the 'keys' to the Kingdom of God.

Karen spent one week within the church of Saint Peter finishing the icon. This enabled the church community to see her at work.

An annotated sketch of Saint Peter in the Desert

Christ hands Peter the 'keys' of heaven but invites him to build the Church on earth. "I will give you the keys of the Kingdom of heaven whatever you bind on earth shall be bound in heaven, whatever you loose on earth will be considered loosed in heaven.'" (Matt 16:19) The Parish of Saint Peter in the Desert has as its Parish Crest a set of keys.

Since the 4th century Peter is portrayed in iconography with a broad rounded face, a short grey beard and short curly hair. I have given him a Roman hairstyle linking him with Rome.

The post-resurrection Peter showing spiritual strength and purpose, who bows his head before the Lord in humble service. His posture shows his response to Christ's question: 'Who do you say I am?' 'You are the Christ.'

In his right hand Peter holds the Church which he was invited to build in the name of Jesus Christ. On the top is a Roman cross.

Peter stands on firm rock not the shifting sand of the desert. Geographically, Saint Peter's Church is built on the firm rock above the sand dunes.

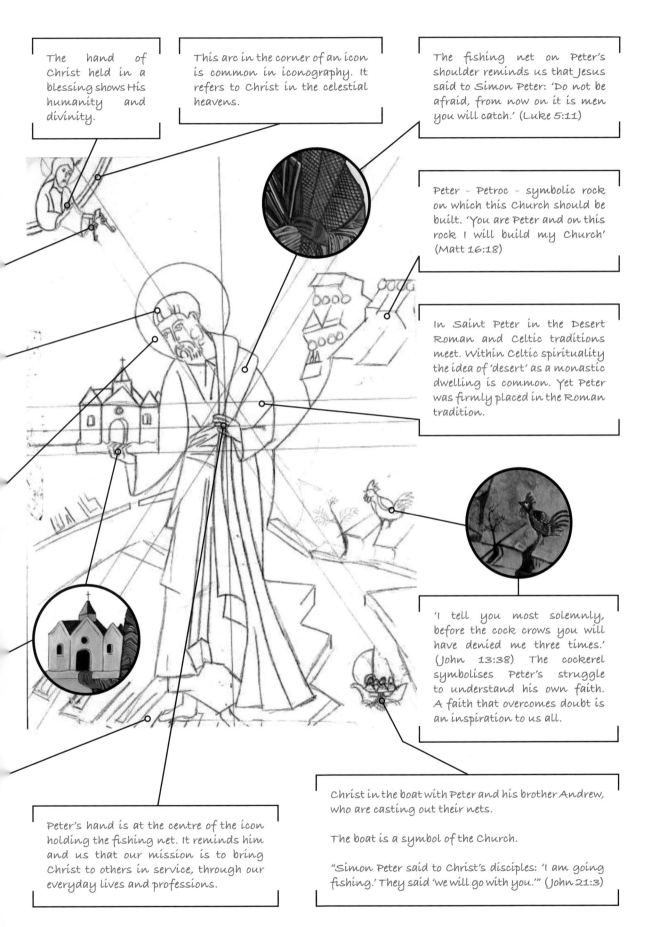

The hand of Christ held in a blessing shows His humanity and divinity.

This arc in the corner of an icon is common in iconography. It refers to Christ in the celestial heavens.

The fishing net on Peter's shoulder reminds us that Jesus said to Simon Peter: 'Do not be afraid, from now on it is men you will catch.' (Luke 5:11)

Peter - Petroc - symbolic rock on which this Church should be built. 'You are Peter and on this rock I will build my Church' (Matt 16:18)

In Saint Peter in the Desert Roman and Celtic traditions meet. Within Celtic spirituality the idea of 'desert' as a monastic dwelling is common. Yet Peter was firmly placed in the Roman tradition.

'I tell you most solemnly, before the cock crows you will have denied me three times.' (John 13:38) The cockerel symbolises Peter's struggle to understand his own faith. A faith that overcomes doubt is an inspiration to us all.

Peter's hand is at the centre of the icon holding the fishing net. It reminds him and us that our mission is to bring Christ to others in service, through our everyday lives and professions.

Christ in the boat with Peter and his brother Andrew, who are casting out their nets.

The boat is a symbol of the Church.

"Simon Peter said to Christ's disciples: 'I am going fishing.' They said 'we will go with you.'" (John 21:3)

Saint Clement de Pierreville

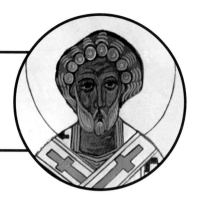

The church and Parish that bear this name have Clement (d.100AD), pope and martyr as Patron Saint. Clement I was the fourth Bishop of Rome after Peter, Linus, and Cletus. The link with Clement and Peter in the name Saint Clement de Pierreville has several possibilities. On a geographical level its location is on the South-East coast of the Island where we find Georgeville, Longueville, Pierreville and Grouville. This may relate to previous Roman villas or small towns.

Within Christian tradition, Peter both baptised and ordained Clement for his life in the priesthood. The Parish of Saint Clement is also noted for its fishing, for which Peter was famous.

Historically, Clement is known mainly for his Epistle to the Corinthians of 96AD. It is a book that focuses on repentance and is an early witness to the authority and function of the ministers of the Christian Church. It shows for the first time a Bishop of Rome intervening effectively in the affairs of another church, and calling for repentance.

According to the 'Acta', a biography of Saint Clement written in the fourth century, he was exiled to the Crimea because he was very good at his job, converting many to Christianity. During his time in exile he was compelled to work in the mines, and is alleged to have opened a miraculous supply of water. In biblical terms this would be seen as him bringing Christ, the living water, to the people of the Crimea. Here he preached with great effect. There were so many converts to Christianity that there was need for seventy-five churches to be built.

However, his zeal also led to his death. He was thrown into the Black Sea with an anchor round his neck, hence the Parish Crest of the anchor.

The final part of his story is very much legend. Angels were said to have made him a tomb on the seabed, and seven centuries later his body was found with the anchor by the missionary brothers, Cyril and Methodius, and returned to his native Rome.

The Parish Church of Saint Clement de Pierreville.

SAINT CLEMENT DE PIERREVILLE

Writing an icon of St Clement de Pierreville

Orthodox iconography has several prototypes for Clement. I chose to depict Clement in his purple crossed garment which highlights his status as Bishop of Rome. The colour purple is mentioned in Scripture; it was a rare and expensive colour only used for kings and emperors. The particular pigment I used in this icon was Alizarin Violet; it takes 24 hours to dissolve in an egg yolk and water mix and results in a vivid purple colour. Purple is a liturgical colour used within the Church at Advent and Lent, times of preparation and repentance. It is a colour fitting for Clement as the letter he wrote to the Coriththians was all about the need for repentance.

The Word of God held in Clement's left hand proclaims the importance of repentance in the plan of salvation. In the top left hand corner of the icon the hand of God in the celestial heavens bestows a blessing on Clement for his ministry on earth.

Within this icon I wanted to show the link between Peter and Clement as the name Saint Clement de Pierreville indicates, so I included a stylised water feature representing the living water with which Peter baptised Clement. It also links Clement's discovery of a miraculous water source, the 'living water', which he subsequently brought to the people of the Crimea.

Clement has distinctive facial features. As in all Orthodox icons they are not humanly expressive but are spiritually revealing. The high convex forehead expresses wisdom and the power of the Holy Spirit. The deep wrinkled cheeks show his ascetic lifestyle. The closed lips indicate that true contemplation requires silence, and the large neck indicates the life-giving breath of the Holy Spirit.

An annotated sketch of Saint Clement de Pierreville

Forehead convex and quite high expressing both power of the Holy Spirit and Wisdom. Cheeks given deep wrinkles to show Clement's ascetic lifestyle. Mouth, fine and geometrical. Lips closed because true contemplation requires silence. Throat and neck disproportionately large to show the life-giving breath of the Holy Spirit.

The hand of Clement held in a blessing. It spells the name of Christ ICXC in whose name the blessing is given.

The harshness of a strange land, symbolising his time in the Crimea.

Arms outstretched in an all-welcoming, protecting gesture. His protecting cape gathers the Christian community.

Clement opened a miraculous water supply while he was in exile in the Crimea. This became a source of living water for the people of the Crimea. Clement set up 75 churches, taking Christ the 'Living Water' to a strange land.

Clement was baptised by Peter.

The sea and seashore show how Clement was killed by being thrown into the sea with an anchor around his neck.

The small purple crosses on the chasuble of Clement proclaim his martyrdom in the name of Christ.

The celestial heavens where Christ resides with all the saints.

The hand of God bestows a blessing on Clement, a martyr in heaven, for the Church on earth.

Clement wrote a letter to the Church in Corinth in 96AD. It refers to the function and authority of the ministers within the Church. In Chapter 7 we read: 'Let us look steadfastly to the blood of Christ, which, having been shed for our salvation has set the grace of repentance before the whole world.' In chapter 5 reference is made to the martyrdom of Peter and Paul.

Vellum cloth was used to hold sacred objects. Here I use it to hold the book Clement wrote.

The church of Saint Clement de Pierreville is a community of believers worshipping God, gathered together in faith, just as Clement gathered together the early Christian community.

Clement's body was found intact in a church built by angels at the bottom of the sea.

Pierreville, the village set up around the church. The community and church act as a safe haven from the sea.

The anchor, the Parish Crest, shows the seafaring people who live in the Parish.

Saint Lawrence

Saint Lawrence was Archdeacon of Rome during the persecution of Christians in the 3rd Century. Lawrence must certainly be one of the most renowned deacons of antiquity. He was known for his charitable service and for his martyrdom four days after the decapitation of his great friend, Pope Sixtus II.

Lawrence was born in Spain in a town near the foot of the Pyrenees, now named Loretto in his honour. While being educated in Gonoa he befriended Sixtus who was a famous and esteemed teacher. Following a migratory wave which was very pronounced at that time, both left Spain for the city where the Apostle Peter had established his See. When Sixtus became Pope, he desired to have Lawrence, his friend and disciple, at his side so as to entrust to him the important office of proto-deacon.

As head deacon of the Church in Rome, Lawrence was known for his subtlety of mind and for his intelligence. He was in charge of the Church's treasure, the sacred vessels and liturgical objects. This is why the Roman soldiers asked Lawrence as keeper of the Church's treasure to hand it over to them. He is said to have asked for a day in which to collect it and then visited the poorest quarters of the city of Rome. He returned the following day to the Roman authorities with a crowd of lame people and beggars and said: "This is the Church's treasure". For this Lawrence was martyred on the 10th August 258 by being roasted on a gridiron. Hence the gridiron is the Parish Crest.

Lawrence is said to have shown no sign of suffering during his martyrdom. He was however, heard to say: "Turn me; I am done on this side."

It was the community of Saint Lawrence that I wanted to involve and recognise in the icon of Saint Lawrence. Through the language of the icon, I wanted to tell the story of Saint Lawrence and his relevance today to the Parish community that bears his name. That is why I depict him with the church of Saint Lawrence in his left hand and a thurible in his right. Both show that as a deacon he was at the service of the Church.

The Parish Church of Saint Lawrence.

SAINT LAURENCE

Writing an icon of St Lawrence

Icons of Saint Lawrence in the Orthodox tradition show him wearing the garments of a deacon, carrying a martyr's cross and a green vellum. In this icon I remain true to the origins of iconography. Lawrence wears garments of a deacon, the white liturgical vestment with the decorated cuff, neck and hem typical of the Church at that time. He also wears the vellum over his left shoulder. He used this to carry the liturgical objects and sacred vessels used in the Church. I have shown Saint Lawrence holding as a sacred vessel the church of Saint Lawrence for all to see. Lawrence's role as deacon would have meant that he was at the service of the Church, not just in liturgical matters but also in the building up of the Church as a religious community.

In the icon is the legendary gridiron, and in the top left hand corner the hand of God can be seen bestowing a blessing on Lawrence, a martyr in heaven for the Church on earth. The two small cameos at the base of the icon tell the story of why Lawrence was martyred.

The other object that Lawrence carries in his left hand is the martyr's cross.

Lawrence's right hand swings the thurible, another symbol of sacrifice (in Greek thurible means to sacrifice). This incense-burner symbolises the prayer of the Saint rising to heaven in the name of the Father, Son and Holy Spirit, hence the 3 chains attached to the thurible. "Let my prayer rise before you like incense." If the eye were to follow the swing of the burner, we see that it would swing towards the gridiron, where his own body was burnt, as an ultimate prayer to God.

An annotated sketch of Saint Lawrence

Lawrence was Archdeacon of Rome. He was born in Spain in 225AD and died a martyr at the age of 33 years. To recognise his time in Rome I have given him a Roman haircut and beard.

Lawrence was roasted on a gridiron. He is said to have shown no sign of suffering. He said to his executioners: 'Turn me, I am done on this side.' The Parish Crest of Saint Lawrence is the gridiron.

Lawrence wears the garments typical of a deacon of his status: the dalmatic – a liturgical vestment worn at mass; the sticharion – a white tunic with a decorated collar, cuffs and hem; the orarion – the deacon's stole was given to him by his friend, Pope Sixtus 11, who was martyred just before Lawrence.

During the persecution of Christians the Roman authorities asked Lawrence, keeper of the Church's treasure, to produce it. Lawrence asked for time to do this and visited the poorest quarters of Rome, collecting beggars and the lame. He returned to the Romans with this crowd of beggars and said: 'These are the Church's treasure.'

In the celestial heavens where God resides with all the saints, the hand of God bestows a blessing on Lawrence, a martyr in heaven for the Church on earth.

The vellum cloth for carrying liturgical objects is worn on the left shoulder. As deacon, Lawrence would use this cloth to hold the sacred vessels which could not be touched by human hands.

Lawrence is entitled to carry the martyr's cross. He is a saint because of his martyrdom and not because he was a deacon.

Lawrence also carries in his left hand the church of Saint Lawrence, a sacred vessel held up for all to see.

The church shows Lawrence's function as a deacon. He was to be at the service of the Church not just in liturgical matters, but also by building up the Church as a worshipping community.

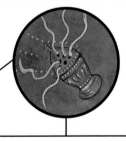

A thurible, incense burner; the smoke symbolises the prayers of the saints rising to heaven. 'Let my prayer rise before you like incense.' The thurible was used by Lawrence during liturgical services, to incense the holy places and at key moments of the liturgy. The word 'thurible' means 'to sacrifice' in Greek. Lawrence sacrifices his life for the Church. The 3 chains attached to the thurible represent God the Father, Son and Holy Spirit.

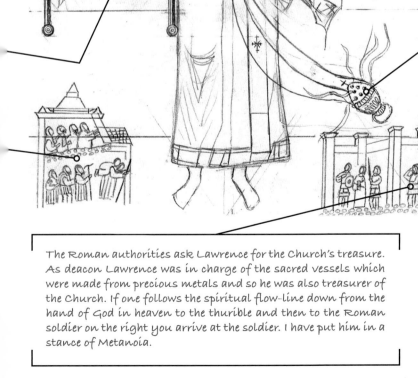

The Roman authorities ask Lawrence for the Church's treasure. As deacon Lawrence was in charge of the sacred vessels which were made from precious metals and so he was also treasurer of the Church. If one follows the spiritual flow-line down from the hand of God in heaven to the thurible and then to the Roman soldier on the right you arrive at the soldier. I have put him in a stance of Metanoia.

Saint Martin de Grouville

Grouville's Patron Saint is Saint Martin de Tours. (316-397) a very popular soldier saint. Martin was born in the town of Sabaria, which at that time was part of the Roman Empire, now known as Hungary. The Parish Crest uses a sequence of 8 red and white or silver stripes; this is taken from the silver of his chain mail and the red of his military cloak which he shared with a beggar.

Martin's father was a senior officer in the Roman army and so he was named after the Roman god of war, Mars. He spent much of his life in what is now France and died at Candes. For this reason Martin is both the Patron Saint of France and of soldiers.

At the age of ten Martin started attending church and his interest in Christianity led him to ask for baptism, but for this he would have to wait. At fifteen he was conscripted into the Roman army, an obligation of a son of an army veteran. He joined the cavalry and was stationed in Amiens, France.

While Martin was at the gates of the city of Amiens he met a beggar. He was so moved that he took off his cloak, cut it in two with his sword, and gave one half to the beggar. At that time half a Roman soldier's uniform was the property of Caesar and half the property of the individual soldier. Martin generously gave away the half that belonged to him.

That night Martin dreamt that Jesus was wearing the half of his cloak that he had given away to the beggar. The dream confirmed to Martin that he should be baptised, and so at the age of eighteen he fulfilled his wish.

After his baptism Martin proclaimed that he had become a soldier for Christ and therefore he could not fight. However, to show he was not a coward he volunteered to go into battle unarmed, but peace was declared and so Martin left the army.

The Parish Church of Saint Martin de Grouville.

SAINT MARTIN DE GROUILLE

Writing an icon of St Martin de Grouville

My challenge was to interpret all this information about the early life of Martin into an icon that was meaningful for Grouville. Since the church, as part of an extension to the church building, had just unearthed Roman remains, I chose to depict Martin as the young Roman soldier. I wanted to capture the event of this life-changing moment for Martin, so I looked for icon prototypes that already showed Martin on his horse at the gates of Amiens.

At the age of 15 years, Martin's gesture shows a young man animated by the Holy Spirit to carry out an act of mercy in the service of God. In the icon the gesture of cutting his cloak in half is big and bold. It was a gesture of charity which changed and shaped the rest of Martin's life. It is also a moment of reflection for the person who gazes upon this icon – a striking reminder that for the Christian, following Christ requires gestures of charity and mercy that turn upside down current egotistic trends.

Pope Benedict XVI said: 'Martin de Tours the soldier who became a monk and bishop, like an icon, illustrates the irreplaceable value placed on individual acts of charity.'

This image shows my original research and drawing for Saint Martin de Grouville.

An annotated sketch of Saint Martin de Grouville

The Celtic symbol of the Trinity. Martin was a pupil of Hillary of Poitiers who was a great believer in the Trinitarian doctrine. He carried this doctrine to the people he met.

I have painted Amiens in blue, symbolic of the Divine. To me Amiens is a symbol of the New Jerusalem. We are reminded in the Gospel passage of John that there are many rooms in my Father's house and all are welcome.

At the age of 15 Martin joined the cavalry and was stationed at Amiens in France. At the age of 18 he was baptised and became a soldier for Christ.

The Parish Crest is a red and silver coat of arms with 8 bars. These colours have been used for the cloak and armour.

At the centre of this icon is the sword. It is symbolic of the two-edged sword of Psalm 149. Martin uses this weapon of destruction in a gesture of charity. He is a model of how Christ invites His followers to perform acts of charity not acts of violence and to turn swords into ploughshares.

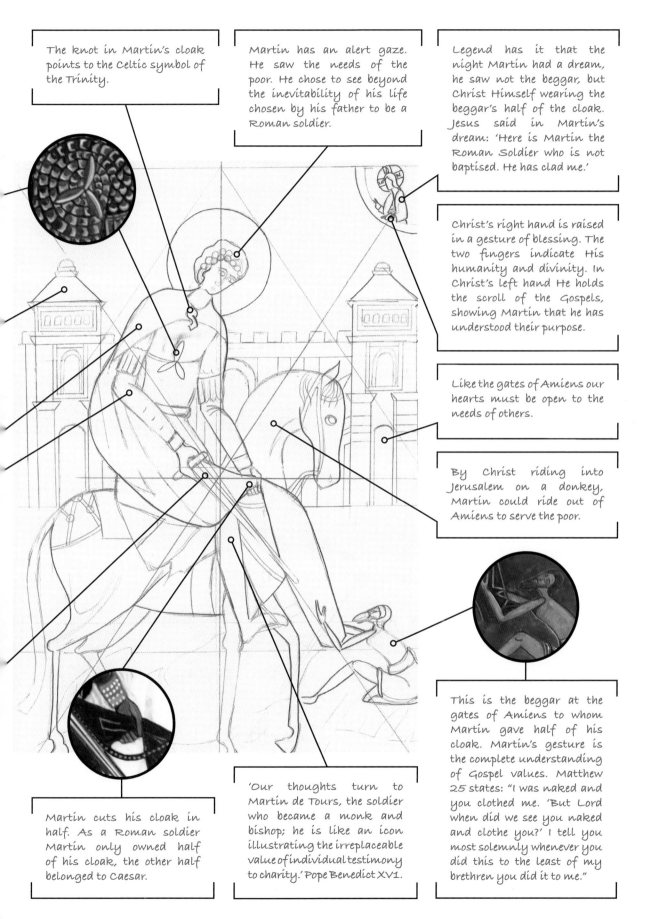

The knot in Martin's cloak points to the Celtic symbol of the Trinity.

Martin has an alert gaze. He saw the needs of the poor. He chose to see beyond the inevitability of his life chosen by his father to be a Roman soldier.

Legend has it that the night Martin had a dream, he saw not the beggar, but Christ Himself wearing the beggar's half of the cloak. Jesus said in Martin's dream: 'Here is Martin the Roman Soldier who is not baptised. He has clad me.'

Christ's right hand is raised in a gesture of blessing. The two fingers indicate His humanity and divinity. In Christ's left hand He holds the scroll of the Gospels, showing Martin that he has understood their purpose.

Like the gates of Amiens our hearts must be open to the needs of others.

By Christ riding into Jerusalem on a donkey, Martin could ride out of Amiens to serve the poor.

This is the beggar at the gates of Amiens to whom Martin gave half of his cloak. Martin's gesture is the complete understanding of Gospel values. Matthew 25 states: "I was naked and you clothed me. 'But Lord when did we see you naked and clothe you?' I tell you most solemnly whenever you did this to the least of my brethren you did it to me."

Martin cuts his cloak in half. As a Roman soldier Martin only owned half of his cloak, the other half belonged to Caesar.

'Our thoughts turn to Martin de Tours, the soldier who became a monk and bishop; he is like an icon illustrating the irreplaceable value of individual testimony to charity.' Pope Benedict XVI.

Saint Martin Le Vieux

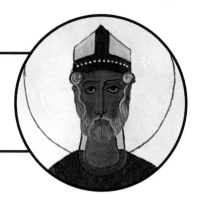

The Patron Saint of Saint Martin Le Vieux is Saint Martin de Tours: the same Patron Saint as for the Parish of Grouville. There are several churches named after Saint Martin de Tours in the East of the Island, probably because of its proximity to France of which Saint Martin is the Patron Saint. Saint Martin Le Vieux, as the name suggests, is the oldest of the eastern Parish Churches.

Saint Martin lived until he was 80 years old, a man of great humility and compassion.

After Martin's baptism he became a pupil of Bishop Hillary of Poitiers and placed himself in this Saint's hands. One night Martin had a dream that his parents would soon die and he received Hillary's blessing to travel to his far-off homeland. There, he had the happiness of seeing his mother's conversion to Christianity before her death. On his way back, he heard that Bishop Hillary had been forced to leave Gaul. Instead of returning there alone, Martin went to an island off the coast of Italy to live a solitary life as a monk until he heard news of St. Hillary's return to Gaul. The two of them then established the first monastery in the West, at Liguge, which grew into a community of hermits and followed the rule of Saint Basil for communal monastic life.

In 371 Saint Martin was again forced to become a guardsman, but this time of the Church. The people elected Martin as Bishop of Tours because of his holiness and life of poverty. Reluctantly Martin accepted to become a bishop but refused to live in a palace. Instead he set up a 'monk's cell' next to the church. Although deeply committed to his responsibilities as a bishop, the constant interruptions caused him to retire from Tours to what was to become the Abbey of Marmoutier.

Martin continued his duties as a bishop with missionary zeal: curing the sick, setting prisoners free, and encouraging those in authority to show mercy. When Martin's final sickness came upon him he was at Candes. He died on the 8th November 397 and was buried at Tours.

The Parish Church of Saint Martin Le Vieux.

SAINT MARTIN LEVIEUX

Writing an icon of St Martin Le Vieux

My challenge was to produce two icons of the same saint. Saint Martin de Tours' early life as a Roman soldier was the theme used for the icon of Saint Martin de Grouville, whereas Saint Martin Le Vieux lent itself to the older man as Bishop of Tours.

Even though this icon depicts Martin as the older man and Bishop of Tours I still wanted Saint Martin to echo his great act of charity, of giving half his cloak to a beggar, in his youth as a Roman soldier. I therefore used the bishop's stole as the focus of the story within the icon.

In Orthodox iconography bishops are sometimes shown with small insets of Christ and Mary. This I have done at the top of the icon. Here, Christ gives Martin the Scriptures, which signifies his authority to preach and teach. Mary gives him the stole of investiture as bishop. Martin's story begins as a young man when he gives half his cloak to a beggar and now in this icon we see the fruits of that gesture as he receives the garment of priesthood in the bishop's stole from Mary the Mother of Jesus.

The chasuble that Martin wears as Bishop of Tours is shaped like a shield and is in the colours of the Parish Crest, red and white.

At the centre of the icon is the Cross, showing in whose name Martin continued to promote the importance of charity in Christian belief. Martin is a great model of the golden rule of Christianity: 'Love one another as I have loved you.'

An annotated sketch of Saint Martin Le Vieux

Christ wears half the cloak that Martin gave to the beggar at the gates of Amiens. The legend says that Martin was spoken to in a dream by Christ Himself: 'Here is Martin, the Roman soldier who is not baptised. He has clad me.'

Christ hands Martin the Book of the Gospels from which a bishop acquires his authority to teach and preach. Martin certainly paid heed to Matthew 25, the passage about Christian charity.

Martin's hand is raised in a gesture of blessing. Its placement in the icon draws the eye to Christ, in whose name Martin blessed his people.

The stylised rock-like mountain, reminds us of Martin's life as a hermit on the island of Gallinaria. The time he spent there enabled him to prepare for his ministry.

The chasuble worn by Martin is in the symbolic shape of a shield. At its centre is the Cross of Christ, just as Christ was at the centre of Martin's life. It is also at the centre of this icon.

The beggar holds up towards Martin half of the cloak he was given in Amiens. His other hand is in an open gesture of acknowledgement and thanks.

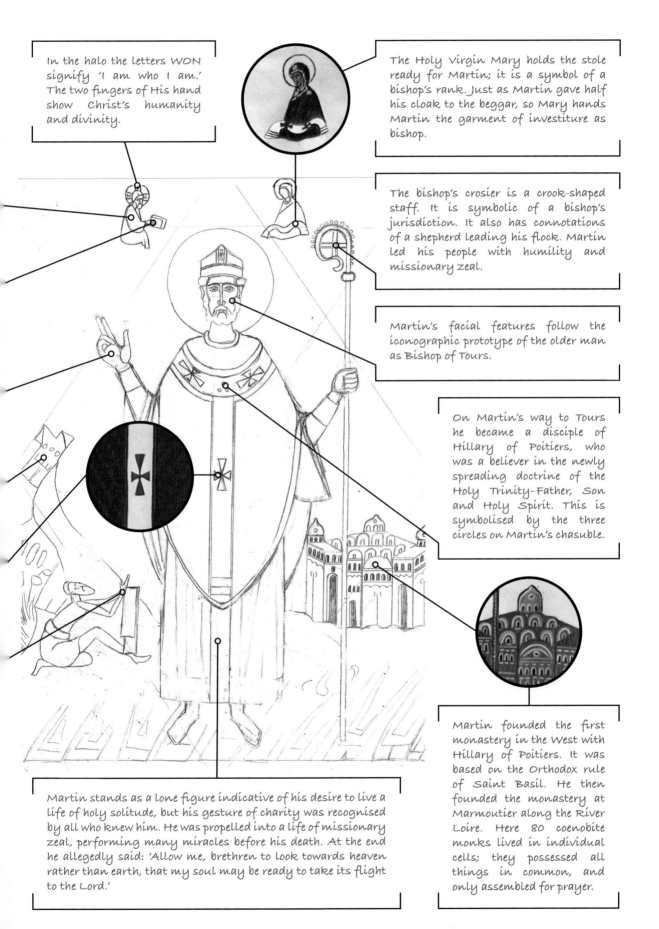

In the halo the letters WON signify 'I am who I am.' The two fingers of His hand show Christ's humanity and divinity.

The Holy Virgin Mary holds the stole ready for Martin; it is a symbol of a bishop's rank. Just as Martin gave half his cloak to the beggar, so Mary hands Martin the garment of investiture as bishop.

The bishop's crosier is a crook-shaped staff. It is symbolic of a bishop's jurisdiction. It also has connotations of a shepherd leading his flock. Martin led his people with humility and missionary zeal.

Martin's facial features follow the iconographic prototype of the older man as Bishop of Tours.

On Martin's way to Tours he became a disciple of Hillary of Poitiers, who was a believer in the newly spreading doctrine of the Holy Trinity–Father, Son and Holy Spirit. This is symbolised by the three circles on Martin's chasuble.

Martin founded the first monastery in the West with Hillary of Poitiers. It was based on the Orthodox rule of Saint Basil. He then founded the monastery at Marmoutier along the River Loire. Here 80 coenobite monks lived in individual cells; they possessed all things in common, and only assembled for prayer.

Martin stands as a lone figure indicative of his desire to live a life of holy solitude, but his gesture of charity was recognised by all who knew him. He was propelled into a life of missionary zeal, performing many miracles before his death. At the end he allegedly said: 'Allow me, brethren to look towards heaven rather than earth, that my soul may be ready to take its flight to the Lord.'

Saint Brelade

Saint Brelade, also known as Branwalder, was the nephew of Saint Patrick. His mother was Dareca, the sister of Patrick. His Father, according to Exeter mythology, was the Cornish King Conan. Brelade, a 6th Century Celtic monk, was educated in Wales before travelling to Dol de Bretagne in France and then to Jersey and Cornwall. He eventually died in Branscombe in Devon.

There has been much confusion over the years as to who was Saint Brelade. During one period in the Island's history, Saint Brelade was confused with Saint Brendan who travelled on the back of a fish; this is why the Parish Crest is the fish. In the icon I have written of Saint Brelade I have included the Parish Crest. Here the fish is Christ Ixthus. The head of the fish looks towards the raised hand of Saint Brelade, which spells the name of Christ. Its gaze passes through the central symbol of the icon, the Celtic cross. This emphasises the type of spirituality and monastic life that Brelade brought to Jersey. The position of the fish forms a protective arc around the boat which carries Saint Brelade towards Jersey.

The Celtic spiritual tradition was closely tied to the Eastern Christian tradition. Saint Brelade as a Celtic monk lived an ascetic lifestyle based on the spirituality of the 4th century Desert Fathers of Egypt. Monks like him often lived in remote places or on rocky islands in their search of voluntary exile, where cold rather than heat was their local penance.

Above the Celtic cross and firmly placed on the Island of Jersey I have included a typical Celtic monastery. Saint Brelade would have lived in a beehive monastery, again based on the Eastern Orthodox tradition; we can find many images of these in icons, and examples of this type of monastic building can be found today in Ireland such as Skellig Michael. These monastic dwellings were known as 'Deserts'.

The Parish Church of Saint Brelade.

Writing an icon of St Brelade

Through the language of the icon, I wanted to tell the story of Saint Brelade and his relevance today to the Parish community that bears his name.

An icon is a window to the Divine. As we look through it, we glimpse statements of faith written in the visual language of the icon.

In the top right hand corner Christ, in the celestial heavens, hands Brelade the Book of the Gospels. On its cover we see the Communicare symbol of the 3 entwined fish representing the Father, Son and Holy Spirit. Christ's left hand is raised in a gesture of blessing. The two fingers indicate both His human and divine nature.

In the icon Saint Brelade stands in the Parish that bears his name on the Island of Jersey. His left hand is open and extended towards Christ to receive the Word of God. His right hand is raised in a gesture of blessing. This hand also spells the name Christ in Greek, ICXC. From this we clearly see the role of Brelade as a Celtic monk spreading the Good News of the Gospels though his lifestyle, even to the Island of Jersey. This is again emphasised by the small boat which represents the Church. The boat heads for Jersey carrying Saint Brelade to these shores. In the boat with him is Saint Samson his friend and companion on many of his journeys. One imagines Saint Samson dropping him off and continuing on to Guernsey, where a parish was founded in his name.

Beehive monastic dwellings as shown in iconographic form. Detail from the icon of The Vision of St Paul -1579 - Solvychegodsk Museum of History and Art, Russia.

An annotated sketch of Saint Brelade

The Saint's right hand is held in a gesture of blessing and spells Christ's name ICXC, in whose name Brelade gives the blessing.

Saint Brelade is surrounded by sea symbolising that he landed on an island but also that his father was the Cornish King Conan, meaning 'of the sea'.

The robe of Saint Brelade is typical of 6th century Celtic monastic dress.

The Celtic cross is at the centre of this icon. It represents the type of spirituality that Saint Brelade brought to Jersey in the 6th Century. It is a three-stepped cross representing Faith, Hope and Charity, the three main virtues of the Christian faith.

Saint Brelade was the nephew of Saint Patrick. His mother was Dareca, the sister of Patrick. He was educated in Wales and travelled to Dol de Bretagne before arriving in Jersey.

Christ in the celestial heavens hands Saint Brelade the Book of the Scriptures. On it is the Saint Brelade Communicare symbol of the three intertwined fish, representing God the Father, Son and Holy Spirit.

Christ's left hand is held in a gesture of bestowing a blessing on Brelade and His two raised fingers symbolise His humanity and divinity.

Celtic monks lived an ascetic tradition which relates back to the first Desert Fathers of Egypt. The beehive hut structures represent the Eastern Orthodox influence on Celtic spirituality. These monastic dwellings were known as 'Deserts', symbolising the austere lifestyle where each monk lived in his own hut and where the monks only met together to eat and worship.

Brelade holds out his left hand to receive the Gospels from Christ.

The fish represents Christ Ixthus. During the Roman persecutions of Christians the fish was a secret symbol used by Christians. Here, the fish shows Saint Brelade the Island of Jersey.

Saint Brelade stands in the Parish that bears his name on the Island of Jersey. Tradition has it that Saint Brelade was Bishop of Jersey.

The boat represents the Church. Here Saint Brelade brings the Gospels to Jersey. With him in the boat is Saint Samson. These two saints frequently travelled together. One can imagine Saint Samson then travelling on to Guernsey.

Saint Helier

Saint Helier was a hermit monk living in Jersey in the 6th century. The church which bears his name has been a place of worship for Christians for over a thousand years. Based on Helier's example of Christian living, the church developed in this area, possibly from a small town gathered around a monastic community, to the present 'Town Church,' which is the seat of the Dean of Jersey and a place for important civic gatherings for the Government of Jersey.

Living within the hermitic tradition, Helier's life was focused on a very austere and ascetic lifestyle. He sought out, like most hermits, a lonely outcrop of rock on which to live a life of prayer, just as the Desert Fathers in the Orthodox tradition sought seclusion in the deserts of Egypt. In Helier's case, cold rather than heat was his penance. The rock at L'Islet surrounded by the sea at high tide was his desert. Here, he hewed out of the rock a bed and ate only once a week in order to starve his human body to feed his soul. This also fed his missionary zeal and he converted many in Jersey to Christianity.

Helier was born in the town of Tongres, in the country we now know as Belgium, in about 510AD. His parents, both pagans, desired a child but this did not happen until Saint Cunibert prayed on their behalf for their marriage to be blessed with a child. However, this was on condition that the child be brought up as a Christian. The hagiography of Saint Helier – 'Acta Sanctorum' or the 'Passion of Saint Helier', – written in 1725, tells us that at the age of 7 years Helier became ill and was paralysed. Again his parents called upon Cunibert for help. Helier was cured and taken by Cunibert into the Church to be educated. Whilst under his influence, Helier began to perform miracles. His parents were unhappy with this and had Cunibert killed. Helier was heartbroken and ran away. However, God directed him towards a holy man called Saint Marculf who baptised him and sent him to our Island of Jersey.

Here, under Marculf's influence, Helier's life as a hermit begins. For about 15 years his life as a Christian was an example to the people of Jersey. In more practical ways, from his vantage point on L'Islet Rock he could look out across the bay and signal to the shore if there were marauding attackers approaching. Finally in 555AD he is said to have been beheaded by one such group of attackers, and despite his frail body, he was able to pick up his head and walk to the shore. He became Jersey's first martyr and it is appropriate that its capital, St Helier, is named after him.

The Parish Church of Saint Helier.

Writing an icon of St Helier

Interpreting all this information about Saint Helier into an icon was challenging, as there were no iconographic prototypes of him because he was a 'local' saint. I therefore looked at how the 'hermit saint' was portrayed in iconography. Several elements seemed to recur, all of them relevant to Saint Helier: a rocky area with a water source and a symbolic cave entrance, and the saint looking up towards some celestial source of inspiration. I also looked at how feeding the soul and not the body was represented in the icon of Mary of Egypt.

My final drawing shows Helier standing in front of his cave, now commonly known as Hermitage Rock. Here I highlight the blue and pink granites of Jersey. His head lies on the seashore and the offending axe is propped up against a rock. Helier wears the robes of an ascetic monk. His cloak is a dark red, the colour worn by martyrs and, as I found on the statue of Saint Helier in Bréville-Sur-Mer, he wears a belt which is tied in a traditional Christian Orthodox way.

Helier's hand gestures sum up his story of holiness and dedication to his faith. One hand points to his decapitated head, and the other is held in an iconographic gesture of a messenger of God. The three fingers, representing God the Father, Son and Holy Spirit, point to the Angel of the Passion carrying the implements of Christ's Passion, a premonition to Helier of his own impending death.

This photograph shows the statue of Saint Helier in the church of Bréville-Sur-Mer in Normandy by kind permission of Roger Sebire.

An annotated sketch of Saint Helier

Helier as a hermit in the tradition of the Desert Fathers, sought out a desert retreat. He found a cave in a crag of a rock cut off by high tide at L'Islet, the tidal island off the south coast of Jersey.

The classic, iconographic style of the entrance to a hermit's cave. Here, it indicates Helier's hermitic lifestyle.

The distinctive beard of Helier points to the centre of this icon. Its shape is taken from the statue of Saint Helier at Bréville-Sur-Mer in Normandy, France.

Helier wears the garments of a hermit monk. These indicate the influences in his life. He wears a dark red cloak, the colour permitted to be worn by a martyr. He was martyred in 555Ad. The Eastern influence can be seen in the Orthodox tie in his belt. Finally the hooded garment shows the Celtic influence, because his teacher Saint Marculf, trained him for three months for his mission in Jersey.

His left hand points to his head lying on the seashore. It shows the consequences of his belief in God and the price he was prepared to pay for saving the people of Jersey from marauding attackers.

The natural causeway which joins the Hermitage Rock to the Island of Jersey.

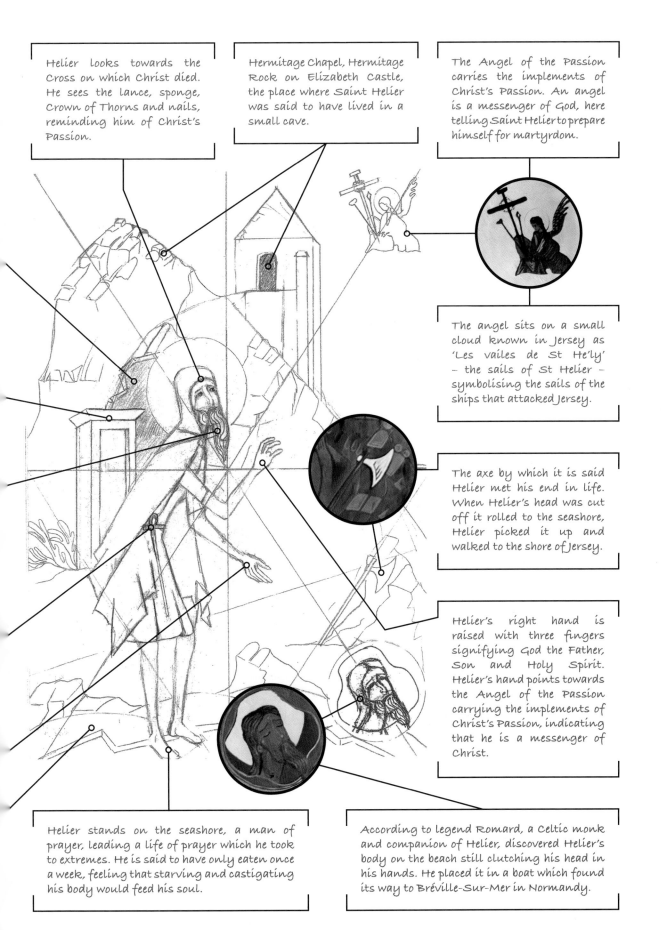

Helier looks towards the Cross on which Christ died. He sees the lance, sponge, Crown of Thorns and nails, reminding him of Christ's Passion.

Hermitage Chapel, Hermitage Rock on Elizabeth Castle, the place where Saint Helier was said to have lived in a small cave.

The Angel of the Passion carries the implements of Christ's Passion. An angel is a messenger of God, here telling Saint Helier to prepare himself for martyrdom.

The angel sits on a small cloud known in Jersey as 'Les vailes de St He'ly' – the sails of St Helier – symbolising the sails of the ships that attacked Jersey.

The axe by which it is said Helier met his end in life. When Helier's head was cut off it rolled to the seashore, Helier picked it up and walked to the shore of Jersey.

Helier's right hand is raised with three fingers signifying God the Father, Son and Holy Spirit. Helier's hand points towards the Angel of the Passion carrying the implements of Christ's Passion, indicating that he is a messenger of Christ.

Helier stands on the seashore, a man of prayer, leading a life of prayer which he took to extremes. He is said to have only eaten once a week, feeling that starving and castigating his body would feed his soul.

According to legend Romard, a Celtic monk and companion of Helier, discovered Helier's body on the beach still clutching his head in his hands. He placed it in a boat which found its way to Bréville-Sur-Mer in Normandy.

Saint Ouen

The Patron Saint of Saint Ouen's Parish Church is Saint Ouen de Rouen (Latin Audaenus). It could be said that he is one of Jersey's most erudite saints. Born into a Gallo-Roman family around 609 in Sancy, France, Ouen's childhood was a privileged one. His father made sure his son was well educated and it seems that Ouen showed a great talent for learning.

Thanks to his education and family status, Ouen was welcomed into the Royal Court of Clothaire II and his successor Dagobert I, who made him chancellor.

Ouen was a devout Christian and wanted to become a monk but Dagobert persuaded him against this. While at the Royal Court, Ouen found a faithful friend, Eloi. Together they served Dagobert, but at his death they both felt released from their duties and left the court.

As a layperson, Ouen began to study theology and actively promoted his Christian religion. He encouraged learning and established several new monasteries.

Ouen was finally ordained a priest in 641 and was consecrated Archbishop of Rouen. He transformed the diocese, ordering worship of false gods to cease. Ouen was known for his austerity and charity. He supported many missionary activities. Shortly after negotiating peace between Neustria and Austrasia in Cologne, he became ill and died at Clichy-la-Garenne on the 24th August 683, the date on which his feast day is now celebrated.

Saint Ouen, who survived Saint Eloi, wrote the biography of his friend. In it he gave valuable information on the moral and religious education of that time. It is one of the most authentic historical documents of the 7th Century.

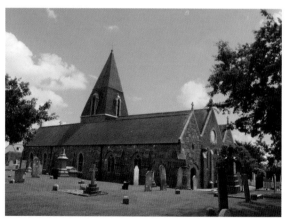

The Parish Church of Saint Ouen.

SAINT OUEN

'WHERE MY FEET
CANNOT TAKE ME
LOVE WILL GUIDE
ME. I WILL GO
WITH DEVOTION
WHERE WORDS
CANNOT ENTER'.
OUEN DE
ROUEN

'TAKE ME
FOR YOUR
MODEL AS
I TAKE
CHRIST'.
1 COR 11:1

Writing an icon of St Ouen

In trying to interpret visually all this historical information about Saint Ouen into an icon, I had to answer some basic questions. What were archbishops wearing in those days? Since Saint Ouen wrote about Saint Eloi, what did 7th Century calligraphy look like? And what did he write about Saint Eloi that could be relevant for today? I found several existing images of Saint Ouen and icons of similar saints of his era. I then did my initial drawings.

I felt it was important to include a scriptorium and a portion of Saint Ouen's 7th Century text in the icon. I also decided to take calligraphy classes so that I could write in the Onciale text of that time.

Looking at the priestly garments I realised that I could include the Parish Crest as a motif on the chasuble. The final drawing conformed to the canons of iconography. The spiritual flow-lines enabled the eye to look at the theological information of the icon, especially the raised hand of Saint Ouen which spells the letters ICXC - Jesus Christ in Greek.

ONCIALE

This is a 7th Century style of calligraphy that Saint Ouen could have used. For this reason I have used it for the written texts in this icon. I have also used it for the title for each one of the Icons of the Twelve Parish Saints.

An annotated sketch of Saint Ouen

Christ hands Ouen the Gospels from which the bishop acquires his authority to preach and teach. Christ's right hand is raised in a gesture of blessing. It also indicates Christ's two natures, His humanity and His divinity.

The hand of Ouen in a blessing spells ICXC echoing the blessing given by Christ to whom he points. This indicates yet again that he takes Christ as his model and it is in Christ's name that he carries out his mission to spread the Gospel.

In iconography the garments worn by bishops are usually very ornate and portray the Cross of Christ. It is for this reason I included the Parish Crest, a yellow cross on a blue background, as a pattern on the Chasuble.

A symbolic monastery indicative of the one Ouen founded, the Abbey of Rabais in 634Ad on land donated by Dagobert 1 and his son Clovis.

The mountain rock is symbolic of the Old Testament idea of climbing a mountain to meet God. Here it shows the seclusion that Ouen sought after his time in the service of Dagobert 1. In quiet reflection he carried out his theological studies.

These garments worn by Saint Ouen are typical of the era of the Court of King Dagobert 1.

The yellow and blue arrows on the mitre of Saint Ouen visually interpret the Scripture text from 1 Corinthians 11:1.

The Virgin Mary holds the stole ready for Ouen, a specific symbol of investiture as bishop, thereby giving him the status of his rank as bishop.

Ouen was chancellor for the Frankish King Dagobert 1. He was born in 609Ad. As a child he was educated at the Abbey of St Médard and became a great statesman. He was known for his austerity and charity.

Ouen wrote one of the most authentic 7th Century historical documents on the Life of Saint Eloi, his friend and colleague. It contains important information on the moral and religious education of that time.

The inverted perspective of the scriptorium is to draw the onlooker into this place of learning and theological study.

The place of the relic. This is to symbolise the 4th Century tradition of sanctifying a place so that a worshipping community could be established. Here a splinter of the bone of Saint Ouen was said to have been obtained for the church of Saint Ouen to be named and dedicated to this Saint. King Harold swore allegiance to the throne of England on the bones of Saint Ouen.

The 'Scriptorium' in this icon is a symbol of Ouen's talent for learning. He not only spent time in study and compiling documents, he also founded places of theological study. He was part of the group charged by Dagobert 1 to compile the Salic Law and he was involved in the Synod of Chalon in 644 to combat simony.

The Holy Trinity

La Sainte Trinité, or the Holy Trinity, is not an individual saint, but a statement of faith. Here we have the great Godhead concept of faith which is usually symbolised in geometrical terms within the Western Christian Church. This theological concept of 'three Persons in one' has been interpreted in a very different way within Eastern Orthodoxy.

This icon prototype is known as 'The Hospitality of Abraham'. Here, three angels visit Abraham and Sarah at the Oak of Mamre. The story of which is found in Genesis chapter 18.

"The Lord appeared to Abraham near the great trees of Mamre while he was sitting at the entrance to his tent in the heat of the day. Abraham looked up and saw three men standing nearby. When he saw them, he hurried from the entrance of his tent to meet them and bowed low to the ground. He said, 'if I have found favour in your eyes, my Lord, do not pass your servant by. Let a little water be brought, and then you may all wash your feet and rest under this tree. Let me get you something to eat, so you can be refreshed and then go on your way – now that you have come to your servant.'. 'Very well,' they answered, 'do as you say.' So Abraham hurried into the tent to Sarah. 'Quick,' he said, 'get three seahs of the finest flour and knead it and bake some bread.' Then he ran to the herd and selected a choice, tender calf and gave it to a servant, who hurried to prepare it. He then brought some curds and milk and the calf that had been prepared, and set these before them. While they ate, he stood near them under a tree."

This very descriptive biblical story lends itself to the visual image of the icon of the Holy Trinity, which in turn leads the Christian believer to a greater understanding of the Godhead.

'Remember to always welcome strangers for by doing this some people have entertained angels without knowing it.' (Hebrews 13:1)

The Holy Trinity Parish Church.

Writing an icon of The Holy Trinity

When reflecting on the icon I would write for the Parish of the Holy Trinity I knew immediately which icon I would create. I would attempt to follow the master of iconography himself, André Rublev. He wrote his own version of this prototype of the Holy Trinity in 1425.

Rublev strips the biblical story of Abraham and Sarah, and the banquet that Sarah prepared for the three strangers under the Oak of Mamre. He stylises the tree, the dwelling of Abraham, and landscape to include the biblical image of a mountain.

What he does is to focus the image to the main statements of faith: God the Father, Son and Holy Spirit.

Above the head of the Father is placed a building symbolising Jerusalem. Above the head of the Son is the tree symbolising the wood of the Cross. Above the head of the Holy Spirit is a stylized mountain, a place of encounter with God. Each angel's hand communicates statements of faith just as each angel's gaze communicates a relationship of love.

To me this icon captures the essence of a Trinitarian faith. There is both unity and diversity held together in Rublev's composition. One can feel the mutual love and the mutual involvement of each Person of the Trinity.

Here we find an invitation for the onlooker to participate in this relationship of love. There is even a place at the table for the believer to sit, and all three angels point to it.

An annotated sketch of The Holy Trinity

The stylized dwelling of Abraham and Sarah becomes the symbol of Jerusalem, the house of God where: 'there are many rooms in the Father's house.' (John 14: 2)

The wings of the angels show that they are divine beings in an earthly encounter.

The angel symbolic of God the Father wears a transparent garment that echoes the idea of the invisible God.

The hand of the Father points both to his Son and the cup of sacrifice, acknowledging the journey that Christ must take to redeem the world.

The hand of Christ indicates His humanity and divinity. He points to the cup with the morsel of lamb, recognizing that Christ was in fact the Sacrificial Lamb of God.

The cup with the sacrificial lamb minimally represents the banquet prepared by Sarah for the three strangers that visit Abraham.

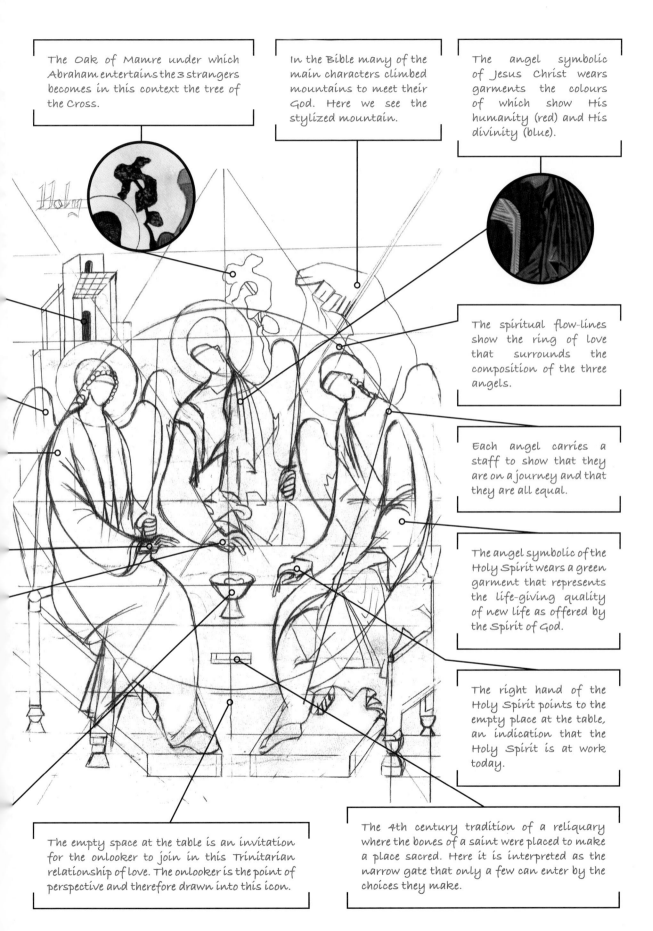

The Oak of Mamre under which Abraham entertains the 3 strangers becomes in this context the tree of the Cross.

In the Bible many of the main characters climbed mountains to meet their God. Here we see the stylized mountain.

The angel symbolic of Jesus Christ wears garments the colours of which show His humanity (red) and His divinity (blue).

The spiritual flow-lines show the ring of love that surrounds the composition of the three angels.

Each angel carries a staff to show that they are on a journey and that they are all equal.

The angel symbolic of the Holy Spirit wears a green garment that represents the life-giving quality of new life as offered by the Spirit of God.

The right hand of the Holy Spirit points to the empty place at the table, an indication that the Holy Spirit is at work today.

The empty space at the table is an invitation for the onlooker to join in this Trinitarian relationship of love. The onlooker is the point of perspective and therefore drawn into this icon.

The 4th century tradition of a reliquary where the bones of a saint were placed to make a place sacred. Here it is interpreted as the narrow gate that only a few can enter by the choices they make.

How the Icons of the 12 Parish Saints were made

Designing and writing the icons of the 12 Parish Saints was a spiritual journey of discovery and encounter. In order to visually interpret each of the Saints I first had to carry out extensive research, explore his or her story and legend and place it in an historical and a scriptural context.

I looked for existing iconographic prototypes of the Saints. These were available for Christ, Mary, John, Peter, Lawrence, Clement and Martin. However, no prototypes existed for local Saints Ouen, Brelade and Helier. So I had to research similar characters or situations: hermits for Helier, 7th century bishops for Ouen and Celtic monks for Brelade. In writing each icon, not only were their stories and legends important, but also the impact of their lives on Christian believers. With the icon of the Holy Trinity, I chose to follow the design and interpretation of Genesis 18 as done by the famous iconographer André Rublev in 1425.

With this research completed I then translated the stories into the language of the icon, and began to write an icon for each of the Saints. The main way in which this was done was through the use of spiritual flow-lines. These spiritual flow-lines create a rhythm to the design, making the icon more dynamic. They define movement and counter movement and hold the design together. They give emphasis to a particular part of the icon and allow for a truly visual exegesis of Scripture. The spiritual flow-lines enable the eye to analyse the main construction of the icon and read the statements of faith found within them.

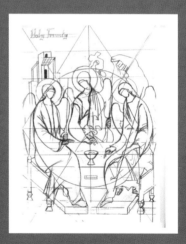

Here is the icon of the Holy Trinity. The spiritual flow-lines are clearly visible.

First I created a story board of all 12 Parish Saints of Jersey.

I endeavoured to write each icon of the Saints, from the 12 ancient Parishes of Jersey, so that they would engage with the reader and give witness to the Christian faith.

The whole process of writing an icon is a Paschal journey, from the bare board of the Crucifixion of Good Friday to the luminous colours of the Resurrection on Easter Sunday.

Crafting the Icon Stage 1

A piece of wood is chosen to make the icon.

A tree has to be chopped down to obtain the wood. The icons of the Twelve Parish Saints are made from recycled pews from Holy Trinity church. The pews were converted into icon boards at the Maritime Museum boatyard.

In the making of an icon the wood is a symbol of the Cross of Jesus Christ.

Crafting the Icon Stage 2

A hollow is carved out of the icon board.

A hollow area is carved out at the centre of the icon board.

This is the sacred place – 'the altar' – where the word of Scripture is written in visual form.

Crafting the Icon Stage 3

The icon board is covered with material.

This is a symbol of the Shroud in which the body of Christ was wrapped and placed in the tomb.

Crafting the Icon Stage 4

The material is covered with a mixture of chalk and rabbit skin glue. This hardens into stone.

This is a symbol of the stone that was rolled in front of the tomb of Christ.

Crafting the Icon Stage 5

The surface of the stone (gesso) is then washed.

This is a symbol of the waters of baptism.

Crafting the Icon Stage 6

The image of the Saint is then engraved onto the stone surface.

This is a symbol of the Word of God written in stone just as the Ten Commandments were carved in stone for eternity.

Gilding the Icon Stage 7

A red clay is then placed on the surface of the gesso as a base for the gold leaf.

In iconography red is the symbol of the earth.

Gilding the Icon Stage 8
The gold leaf is then placed onto the red clay.

This is a symbol of the presence of God.

Painting the Icon Stage 9
The paint mixture is made using egg yolk, water and vinegar. The egg mixture is then mixed with the different colour pigments.

Egg tempera is the binding medium used for the pigments. The yolk of an egg, which has the potential for life, is mixed with water and vinegar, a reminder of the Crucifixion. This egg and pigment mixture petrifies and becomes everlasting.

Painting the Icon Stage 10
The pigments are then painted onto the icon, the darker colours first then the lighter ones.

This symbolises climbing the mountain of the Transfiguration towards the glory of God. The final white lightning flashes of paint symbolise the white Resurrection garments of Christ.

Selected Bibliography

Babic Gordana, *Icons*.
(Studio Editions, 1988)

Brown Raymond E., Fitzmyer Joseph A.,
Murphy Roland E. (Editors)
The New Jerome Biblical Commentary. Student Edition.
(Geoffrey Chapman, 1993)

Castle Tony, *Gateway to the Trinity*.
(St Pauls, 1993)

Castleden Rodney, *The Book of Saints*.
(Quercus Publishing, 2006)

Ewen A. H., de Carteret A. M.
Fief of Sark.
(Guernsey Press 1969)

Haustein-Bartsch Eva, *Icons*.
(Taschen, 2008)

Holy Bible, New Revised Standard Version.
(Oxford University Press, 1989)

Le Diraison-Maxime, Article: *Brittany's Celtic Past*.
(A Journal of Orthodox Faith and Culture, Road to
Emmaus. Vol. IV, No 4.)

Livingstone E.A. (Editor of Third Edition),
The Oxford Dictionary of the Christian Church.
(Oxford University Press, 1997)

McManners John (Editor),
The Oxford History of Christianity.
(Oxford University Press, 1993)

Ouspensky Leonid, *Theology of the Icon Volume I*.
(St Vladimir's Seminary Press, 1992)

Quenot Michel, *The Icon: Window on the Kingdom*.
(St Vladimir's Seminary Press, 1991)

Roozemond-van Ginhoven Hetty J.,
Ikon Inspired Art Icons from "De Wijenburg".
(Wijenburg Foundation, 1980)

Stevens Charles, Arthur Jean, Stevens Joan
Jersey Place Names.
(Société Jersiaise, 1986)

Sr. Petra Clare, *Course Notes*.
Sancti Angeli Benedictine Skete.

Syvret Marguerite, Stevens Joan,
Balleine's History of Jersey.
(Phillimore & Co Ltd for Société Jersiaise, 1998)

Tradigo Alfredo, *Icônes et Saints D'Orient*.
(Editions Hazan, 2005)

Vicini Anna, (Notes on Icons),
Icons & Holiness.
(St Paul Media Productions, 1991)

Vicini Anna, (Notes on Icons),
Symbols of Glory.
(St Paul Media Productions, 1992)

Vicini Anna, (Notes on Icons),
The Flame of the Eternal.
(St Paul Media Productions, 1993)

Williams Rowan,
The Dwelling of the Light: Praying with Icons of Christ.
(Canterbury Press Norwich, 2003)

Revd Monk Dr. Gozard Essay on Celtic Christian Spirituality.
Accessed on *www.orthodoxinfo.com*

The on-line Catholic Encyclopaedia
www.newadvent.org

Butler Alban Rev. The Lives of the Fathers, Martyrs, and
Other Principal Saints (James Duffy, 1866,) website 2010
www.bartleby.com

Letter of St Clement to the Church in Corinth
www.earlychristianwritings.com

Parish Saints research
www.societe-jersiaise.org